The Only Way is Ethics

Sexual Singleness

Why singleness is good, and practical thoughts on being single and sexual

Sean Doherty

First published 2015 by Authentic Media Limited,
52 Presley Way, Crownhill, Milton Keynes, MK8 0ES.
authenticmedia.co.uk

British Library Cataloguing in Publication Data
A catalogue record for this book is available from the British Library.
ISBN 978-1-78078-148-8
E-book ISBN 978-1-78078-437-3

Cover design by Sara Garcia

Singleness is not an academic issue for me. Soon after I became a Christian, I realised that I was gay. I was part of a wonderful youth congregation that did not shy away from teaching about real life issues, and pretty quickly I got the message that it was OK to be gay, but that I shouldn't act on my sexual orientation: sex is a good gift, but only to be used in marriage between a man and a woman. So I assumed that I would remain single for life.

Here, I'll unpack some theology that explains why singleness is hard, but also why it can be deeply fulfilling and needs to be valued much more highly by the church. In fact, I'm going to argue that singleness is *better* than marriage – not a standard view in church! I'll look at the question of whether Jesus was single, and show how we all need intimate friendship in order to be fulfilled. Then I'll take this theology and apply it to some really practical questions, such as whether Christians should marry non-Christians, how you can be sexual without having sex, masturbation, living a fulfilled life whatever your situation, and how the church can value and support single people better. Let's kick off by looking at why singleness is so hard in the first place.

Why is singleness as a Christian so hard today?

Many people think it's preposterous, even dangerous to go without sex. They believe that sex is just a consensual arrangement between two adults for mutual enjoyment – and an inherent part of being fulfilled. This view puts pressure on single Christians who seek to live within the classic Christian belief that sex is a gift for marriage. Movies such as *The 40-Year-Old Virgin* mock the idea of someone reaching the age of 40 without ever having this supposedly essential human experience.[1]

And in church, many single Christians feel abnormal for not being married. Leadership may be based around couples, and churches may emphasise 'family' ministry, even holding 'family services' (also painful for couples dealing with infertility). Some churches run marriage courses, provide marriage preparation, and publicly congratulate people when they get engaged – but where is the equivalent investment in and celebration of living well as a single person? Even (urgently needed) teaching on godly dating and relationships can make it seem as if the goal is to escape singleness by getting married.

The message from the church seems to be that marriage is the norm and singleness is a temporary state on the way. Many people therefore feel marginalised, as if they are a spare 'half' waiting around for someone else to complete them. This is an unrealistic prospect for many Christian women, because the church has far more single women members than men.

Of course, many people are single because they are divorced or their spouse has died. And some Christians remain single because of their sexuality – they are not attracted to anyone of the opposite sex and are committed to remaining celibate.

---

[1] *The 40-Year-Old Virgin*, dir. Judd Apatow, (Universal Pictures, 2005).

So, single Christians are caught between a rock and a hard place: trying to be sexually pure in a sex-obsessed world, and trying to be fulfilled in a church that seems obsessed with marriage.[2] We have to do better than this!

Is singleness meant to be this hard?

The pressure many single people in the church feel to marry (and the sense of failure and incompleteness they may feel if they don't) is unfair and unnecessary. Embracing a more biblical theology of sex and singleness would alleviate this. But whilst we need to become more positive about singleness, we must not deny how hard it can be. I recently visited a church to preach about homosexuality, and in doing so spoke positively about singleness, wanting to affirm and honour those who are living this way. But a woman said afterwards that I had caused her pain. In my rush to affirm the goodness of singleness, I had skated over its challenge and cost.

The Bible gives a reason for this heartache. Although everything that God makes is 'very good' (Gen. 1:31), Genesis 2 identifies a seeming lack in what God has made: 'It is not good that the man should be alone' (v. 18). Humanity is not designed for solitude, but for relationship and community. Thus, here is the element of truth in the idea that marriage is the norm or ideal: at this stage in God's unfolding plan for the world, marriage (and procreation) gives the primary solution to the problem of human solitude. This is

---

[2]For more on this theme, I recommend the brilliant book by my friend Kate Wharton, *Single Minded: Being Single, Whole and Living Life to the Full* (Oxford: Monarch, 2013), ch. 2 – 4.

why the majority of single people would prefer to be married, having one particular person with whom to share their lives. We should dwell on this point for two reasons.

First, we see that even though the Bible teaches that singleness is very good, it is costly. Not only because single people experience pressure from the church and the world, but also because God made us for an intimate relationship with another person. He made our bodies for sex and our hearts for love. So, singleness can be wonderful, and used by God, but it can involve loneliness and unfulfilled sexual desire and hopes, such as to have children.[3] Of course, marriage is also very challenging. Most married people experience loneliness at times, and some chronically. Some married couples have unfulfilled hopes for children as well. But no matter how much single people have good friends and community around them, they still face the particular cost of singleness in terms of sexual abstinence and not having one particular person who is committed to them for life.

The second point about Genesis 2:18 is more surprising: *God is not enough for us.* God does not say, 'it is not good that the man should be alone; I had better stick around,' but, 'I will make him a companion.'[4] Some

---

[3]See 'Sex and the Single Woman' by Fabienne Harford, online at http://www.thegospelcoalition.org/article/sex-and-the-single-woman.

[4]My translation. Although the Hebrew word *ezer* can be translated 'helper', this sounds as though Eve's role is to serve Adam. But *ezer* usually refers to God as the 'helper' of Israel, so it certainly does not imply subordination.

Christians believe that they must find fulfilment in God alone, an idea that has crept into the lyrics of quite a few worship songs. So, when I was single, I thought that the solution to loneliness was to keep growing in my intimacy and relationship with God. That helped, of course. But as I drew closer to God, I discovered something I didn't expect: God was not enough! I needed to be close to other humans too, because God made us to need and care for one another. This is part of what makes us truly human.

Was Jesus single?

So, the Bible explains why singleness is hard. But keep turning the pages of the Bible and you'll discover that is not the whole story. Marriage is good, but it is not the only route to fulfilment. The most powerful reason to believe this, is the life and example of Jesus.

Jesus probably never married.[5] If he did, why did the writers of all four gospels think it was so unimportant that they never bothered to mention it? They tell us about his parents, his relatives (Elizabeth, Zechariah and John the Baptist), the way Mary and Joseph discovered Mary's pregnancy, Jesus's birth, and the fact that he had brothers and sisters (Mark 6:3 even gives his brothers' names). The early church was a family affair – Jesus's mother Mary, and one or two of his brothers (James and perhaps Jude) were prominent within it.

Singleness was very unusual for a rabbi of Jesus's day. So if he had been married, the church would not have

---

[5] I am grateful to Dr Ian Paul, who helped me develop these arguments.

needed to cover it up. And, as we shall see, Jesus being single fits well with his own teaching about marriage, which was very radical. So, whilst we can't totally prove that Jesus was single, it seems very likely that the gospels would have mentioned his wife and children if he'd had any.

Singleness and fulfilment

So Jesus was probably unmarried. Paul was *definitely* unmarried (at least when he wrote 1 Corinthians), and he intended to stay that way. So the New Testament is dominated by single people! But in the Jewish and Roman context of Jesus and Paul, singleness was much more unusual than today. Marriage was compulsory under Roman law (otherwise Roman men just enjoyed casual affairs and never got round to having legitimate heirs). Having children was a public duty! Marriage was not compulsory in Judaism, but singleness was very unusual because the Old Testament valued marriage and procreation so highly.

Yet it seems obvious that Jesus was more fulfilled than you and me. If not, why follow him? Indeed, he lived the most fulfilled life possible. So, being human and fulfilled does not have to include marriage and sex. Jesus lived the most fulfilled life that has ever been lived without either.

And, as we will see, Jesus taught that in the new creation, even though we will still be physical, bodily creatures, and we will still be men and women, marriage and sex will not exist. Yet we will be perfectly fulfilled without them. We won't miss sex!

This is a development from the Old Testament. There, we saw that marriage is God's primary answer to human solitude. But in the New Testament, sex and marriage are not necessary for fulfilment. Sure, sex is nice. And singleness can be hard. But Jesus shows us that you can live a deeply fulfilled life (I didn't say an easy life) without sex and marriage.

Friendship and intimacy

Jesus shows us that we can be fulfilled without sex. But we can't be fulfilled without *intimacy*. Jesus might not have been married, but he needed family and friends. God becoming human meant being born into a normal family. Jesus was vulnerable and dependent on others for his physical and emotional needs.

This is equally true in Jesus's adult life. Although he ministered to multitudes and had many encounters with individuals, Jesus deliberately ordered his life around a small group of people – not servants, but friends (John 15:13–15). They ate together and shared their money. Even when Jesus sent his friends out on mission, he sent them in pairs, not alone (Mark 6:7).

Amongst his twelve closest followers, Jesus had a particular inner circle of three (Peter, James and John). This privileged relationship was partly a matter of teaching and training them, but they were also the ones he wanted with him for company and prayerful support in his agonising distress in Gethsemane (Matt. 26:37).

One friend was so close to Jesus that this friend describes himself as 'the disciple whom Jesus loved' (e.g. John 20:2). Jesus confides the identity of his betrayer to the beloved disciple (John 13:23 – note that Peter, the leader, knows that the best way to get this information from Jesus is to ask this disciple). And when Jesus is dying, it's the beloved disciple he asks to look after his mother (John 19:26–27). We find the 'beloved' description confusing, because Jesus loves everyone! But Jesus still needed friends to help him and to share with, just like the rest of us.

Some people today speculate that this deep same-sex friendship must have been a homoerotic or sexual one. This says more about our obsession with sex than about the reality of the friendship. Indeed, many in the ancient world believed that friendship between two men could be far closer than between a married couple, so we're mistaken to read sexual undertones into the fact that Jesus 'loved' this disciple.

This matters, because our tendency to see intimacy in sexual terms makes it harder for us to form deep friendships. We fear that our feelings will become sexual, or that our friendship will be misinterpreted. Because of my sexuality, I used to hold back from deep friendships with other guys, partly because I was scared I might develop feelings for them. (I now tease my male friends that I solve this by only having ugly friends.) Similarly, I believe that straight people of the opposite sex can have close friendships – just as Jesus formed friendships with women as well as men (Mary and Martha in John 11:5 and Luke 10:38–42). Of course, if you really have the hots for someone, it would be dumb to seek a deep friendship with them. And sometimes two friends develop an inappropriate attraction. But that can be dealt with through honesty,

sensible boundaries and good accountability. We can't let
the mere possibility hold us back from deep friendships.

Our tendency to see intimate relationships in sexual
terms can even hinder friendship between straight people
of the same sex. I know a single woman who had a close
female friend who was teased by other Christians for
having a so-called girlfriend. Yet here were two people
seeking to live godly and fulfilling lives. Their friendship
helped them do this. They should have been applauded
as a good example, rather than treated with suspicion.
This will only put people off friendship. Married or single,
we *all* need friendship. But intentionally cultivating this
life-sharing friendship is particularly essential for single
people, and we'll look at this more below.

The Church is our true and eternal family

Jesus lived a fulfilled life in friendship and community. He
did not dismiss marriage and family life, but the community
he formed around himself was much more important: the
church. Shockingly, for a Jew of his day, when members of
his human family were waiting outside to see him, he did
this: 'Looking about at those who sat around him, he said,
"Here are my mother and my brothers! For whoever does
the will of God, he is my brother and sister and mother"'
(Mark 3:34–35). He ignores his family, and says that they are
not really his family! Our human family may be good, bad
or ugly (or usually a mix of all three), but the church is now
our true family and our primary human community.

Jesus also taught that marriage is fundamentally temporary. Some Sadducees (who did not believe in the

resurrection) presented a scenario to Jesus in which a woman married seven men. They asked, 'In the resurrection, therefore, of the seven, whose wife will she be?' (Matt.22:28). Jesus retorted, 'In the resurrection they neither marry nor are given in marriage, but are like angels in heaven' (v. 30). Marriage is good, but temporary.

This is because part of the purpose of marriage is to reflect the relationship between Christ and the church (e.g. Eph. 5:31–32). When Jesus returns, the union between Jesus and his people will be perfected, so we won't need marriage to point to it. So, marriage is temporary, but the church is eternal.

This perspective made the early church very radical. People who were seen as inferior by wider society, such as women, slaves and the poor, were meant to be treated equally to rich free men. Fellow Christians were 'brothers and sisters'. Churches usually met in houses, and Peter and Paul describe the church as an *oikos* – a household or family. This even means that Christians should show one another physical affection, and several times Paul instructs people to 'greet one another with a holy kiss' (e.g. Rom. 16:16). This seems normal to us – but it was very strange in his day to encourage physical touch between people who were not related to one another. But they *were* related, through Christ.

This challenges us all. Married people: do you get your sense of identity and security from the fact that you are married? When I'm having a bad day, it is easy to expect my wife to cheer me up, or to think, 'At least my kids love me!' And it is good and natural to receive love and support this way. But it is easy to idolise these good things if they eclipse my primary identity as a child of God and part of Jesus's body. It is easy to hold back from serving in church because of my family commitments, or never to make time for other friends. Plus, it puts unfair pressure on my family to meet all my needs.

And if you are single, it is not wrong to want to be married. But keep it in perspective. It's tempting to yearn for marriage so much that you forget you are *already* part of the most important and fulfilling human community. Marriage does not solve anyone's problems or make life easier, nor can it bring ultimate fulfilment. Just as I can treat my family as an idol, so the search for a partner can become a distraction from our primary community, the church. It is not wrong to want one special person with whom to share your life. But one person is not enough. Even God always has two! That's why we need church.

Marriage is good - but singleness is better

The New Testament goes even further than this. Marriage is still seen as good – it reflects the way God originally made us. But singleness is better, because it anticipates the new creation. It foreshadows and lives out a little bit of eternity here and now. (Saying singleness is better is not the same as saying that singleness is easy!)

Paul teaches directly that singleness is better than marriage. In 1 Corinthians 7 he begins, 'It is good for a man not to have sexual relations with a woman' (v. 1). He may be quoting from a letter *from* the Corinthians. Some of them believed that being spiritual meant avoiding supposedly nasty physical things like sex. (Others went to the opposite extreme of believing they could do what they liked with their bodies and it wouldn't affect them spiritually.) So, Paul reminds married couples not to give up sex, except temporarily and by mutual agreement (v. 5).

So, Paul is not against marriage and sex. But note why he thinks someone should marry: 'If they cannot exercise self-control, they should marry. For it is better to marry than to burn with passion' (v. 9). This is hardly a ringing endorsement! Paul is not encouraging marriage for its own sake so much as saying that marriage is better than sexual sin (see v. 2: 'because of the temptation to sexual immorality, each man should have his own wife and each woman her own husband').

But Paul's real preference is singleness: 'I wish that all were as I myself am' (v. 7). Nobody is obliged to be single, but it is better. Of course, if you are already married, you must stay that way: everyone should 'remain in the condition' in which they were when they became Christians (v. 20). So single people should seek to remain single, unless they cannot control themselves sexually (although this category includes nearly everyone at one time or another).

What about people who are betrothed? Again, it is better for them not to marry, because of the imminent return of Jesus: 'for the present form of this world is passing away' (v. 31). The new creation is on its way, when there will be no marriage. Jesus's return has only grown nearer since then.

Paul then explains why singleness is better than marriage: single people are less burdened by worldly anxieties and can focus on serving God more wholeheartedly. 'The married man is anxious about worldly things, how to please his wife, and his interests are divided. And the unmarried or betrothed woman is anxious about the things of the Lord, how to be holy in body and spirit' (vv. 33–34). Marriage is good, but a potential distraction. So singleness is better, if you can keep your sexual desires under control. It enables an 'undivided devotion to the Lord' (v. 35) – which we see in the many single people who have made a remarkable impact for God in mission, prayer, theology and so on.

As theologian and musician Kathryn Wehr points out, in the early church some thought that this was why Jesus said resurrected humanity would be 'like angels'. Angels are completely tuned in to God and surrendered to his will. They are able to do what he wants right away.[6] Paul concludes, 'So then he who marries his betrothed does well, and he who refrains from marriage will do even better' (v. 38). Marriage is good – but singleness is better.

As promised, it's now time to take the theology we've looked at and see how it applies to the big practical questions of singleness. And one of the most challenging is whether Christians should only marry one another. Let's start with that.

Should Christians only marry other Christians?

In 1 Corinthians 7:39 we find the clearest statement in the New Testament that Christians should only marry other

---

[6]Kathryn Wehr, *Singleness and the Early Church: Encouragement for Living the Single Life in Christ Today* (Cambridge: Grove, 2012), pp. 7–8.

Christians: 'A wife is bound to her husband as long as he lives. But if her husband dies, she is free to be married to whom she wishes, only in the Lord.'

First, the good news. As we've seen, the New Testament introduces significant freedom to the question of whether you should get married. Each person, under God, must discern their own calling. Similarly, here Paul emphasises our freedom over whom to marry: 'to whom she wishes'. I am not saying that arranged marriages are completely prohibited. But even when an arranged marriage has been proposed, the couple themselves must still make up their own minds.

Now the challenging news: Paul does specify that a believer with this free choice should only marry another believer, 'in the Lord', although if a Christian does get married to a non-Christian, Paul is clear that such marriages are completely valid marriages (vv. 12–16).

My wife and I are both Christians. And our marriage takes hard work: on communication, making sacrifices, facing tricky decisions, forgiving each other, and so on. And that is with a committed fellow Christian. Of course many non-Christians are very supportive of their spouse's faith, nevertheless living life with someone who does not ultimately share your values and understand you at your deepest level definitely adds a layer of complexity for most people.

Of course, this advice may seem fatuous to many single Christians, especially women, because they do not have the luxury of choosing between singleness and marriage to a Christian. They may feel, as Paul says elsewhere, that 'it is better to marry than to burn with passion' (1 Cor. 7:9). This brings us to the crucial question of what to do with unfulfilled sexual desire, as a single person.

Being single and sexual

There is no point pretending that living without sex is easy. For most single people, sexual abstinence sometimes or often leads to physical and emotional frustration which can be very intense. Some friends and I run a website called 'Living Out', the subject of which is ostensibly homosexuality. But the most frequently viewed page, written by my friend Ed Shaw, is entitled, 'How can you live life without sex?'[7] Plenty of straight people are asking that question too.

It may help to remember that being a sexual person is not just about whether you have sex or not. People who believe that sex is for marriage can end up running away from or scared of the fact that they are *already* sexual beings as women and men. Sexuality is about a lot more than our genitalia: it affects the way we dress and present ourselves to others, the way we interact with other people, our sense of identity.

For example, every so often my wife goes out with 'the girls'. She has a bath, chooses nice clothes and puts on jewellery and make-up. These things help her look and feel good about herself and her body. They express and celebrate her sexuality, but they have nothing to do with having sex.

---

[7]Ed Shaw, 'How can you live life without sex?' online at http://www.livingout.org/how-can-you-live-life-without-sex-.

Jesus himself was a sexual being. In becoming fully human, by definition he had to become either male or female. Being sexual is not sinful – and you are sexual whether you actually have sex or not. Recognising this provides a healthy basis for sexual self-acceptance. Your sexuality mustn't be repressed, but *integrated* with your faith. I share how this worked out in my own life in *Living Out My Story*. See also 'Go Deeper' at the end of this discussion for resources with more practical guidance on this.

Masturbation

Masturbation causes a huge amount of guilt and shame for many people (married and single). Is masturbation a legitimate, healthy release of sexual desire when it has nowhere else to go, or a sinful and selfish transgression of sexual boundaries?

See the next page for what the Bible has to say about masturbation:

[This page intentionally left blank]

That is, the Bible never says that masturbation is a sin. Some have fancifully read this into the episode of Onan spilling his semen on the ground (Gen. 38:9), but Onan's sin was trying to prevent his brother from having an heir by using the withdrawal method of contraception. The Law refers rather quaintly to men having 'nocturnal emissions' (Deut. 23:10). This could refer to spontaneous ejaculation (wet dreams), or it could be a reference to masturbation. If so, it's significant that the Law doesn't treat it as a sin, but as a ceremonial impurity.

Of course, silence on an issue in the Bible does not automatically mean it is OK. If it is a form of sex outside marriage, then it is an abuse of the gift of sex. It is taking sexual pleasure for oneself without any of the commitment to and care for another person that sex within marriage involves. But if masturbation is such a heinous sin, I still find it surprising that the Bible never troubles to say so.

But God is unambiguously opposed to lust. Jesus said: 'Everyone who looks at a woman with lustful intent has already committed adultery with her in his heart' (Matt. 5:28). Lust demeans a precious person who has been created in God's image. It treats them as an object for your own gratification. And, in a day when pornography is available at the click of a button, lust is clearly a huge temptation. Perhaps masturbation without lust is possible purely as a physical release of sexual tension. But lust and masturbation are usually very closely connected. Rather than relieving lustful desire, it can also stimulate it. So, whilst I am reluctant to say outright that masturbation is a sin, it could be playing with fire, and hinder the pursuit of a healthy, integrated sexuality.

From theology to reality: some practical suggestions

I want to conclude by suggesting some ways in which the theology I have outlined can make a positive, practical difference. I write this with trepidation, aware that it has been quite a while since I was single (although, as I share in *Living Out My Story*, I thought I would be single for life).

1. Live life to the full, whatever your situation

Try asking yourself this question. If God/an angel/the Bible[8] suddenly told you that you were going to remain single for the rest of your life, how would it affect your life? Would you live your life differently? Are there dreams or callings that you have been putting on hold until you knew whether or not you would get married?

Maybe you wouldn't do anything differently. Or maybe you would get on with certain things, make different choices about where you live, what you do, church involvement, family life and friendships. Don't miss out on anything that God has for you because you are waiting to get married first. See marriage as a bonus, not as a prerequisite for living fully. If you don't get married, that could still be painful, but at least you won't be missing out on living life to the full. Don't keep a 'hope chest' under your bed, literally or metaphorically – just get it out and start enjoying life.

I have friends who felt called to adopt children when they were single. They wanted to get married but they

---

[8]Select according to your theological preference.

refused to wait around, in case it didn't ever happen. Of course, not everyone is called to parent on their own. But the principle is: don't let being single hold you back from fulfilling God's call, whatever that might be for you. Sometimes marriage even makes things harder, not easier.

If having a relationship or getting married is your goal, singleness can only be about coping as best you can, for as short a time as possible. Learning to live a content and full life will benefit any future marriage anyway. But getting married in order to escape from some perceived deficit will not solve any problems – it will just inflict them onto someone else!

2. Healthy and fulfilled singleness doesn't just happen

Many churches run marriage preparation courses, marriage retreats, marriage this, that and the other. We recognise that marriage needs good preparation and ongoing investment. Here's the big secret: *so does singleness.*

A friend once said to me, 'I just wish I knew one way or another whether I would get married or not. If I knew I would stay single, I would be disappointed, but I could grieve and move on. It would be so much easier to plan out my life if I just knew.' When I thought I was going to be single permanently, that forced me to work out what I would need and intentionally seek support from friends and mentors.

Again, if you knew you were going to stay single, how would you prepare and what would you need? Examples might include who you live with, where you live, the kind of work you do, involvement in church and ministry, healthy physical touch, having a mentor or spiritual director, fun and leisure, feeling appreciated and valued, spending time on your own and spending time with others, and so on. It is healthy and right to seek out good ways of meeting these legitimate needs.

3. You can live without sex, but you can't live without intimacy

A few godly and gifted people are able to live a sex-ually pure life in isolation. But most of us need help! In Christianity, people committed to celibacy usually joined a community of other celibates. This is partly in order to have accountability and support in the battle for purity. But more importantly, it is because we all need people to share our lives with. That is how God made us.

Once when preaching I talked about needing deep friendships. But someone pointed out to me afterwards that depth is not enough. She had deep friendships. What she missed was someone to share shallow things with. Maybe 80 per cent of marriage is the 'shallow' stuff: empt-ying the dishwasher, sharing how your day went, watch-ing a movie, knowing someone will miss you when you're away. Intimacy is built on small things.

Living well as a single person means sharing life with others on a day-to-day basis. This was exactly what Jesus did. As Mark's gospel puts it, Jesus 'appointed twelve . . . *so that they might be with him* and he might send them out to preach' (3:14, my emphasis). Jesus did not gather disciples just so he could send them to preach. First and foremost they were called to 'be with him', to share life together.

I think this is the single biggest change we need to make in church. Rather than seeing singleness as being on your own and marriage as being together, everyone needs people with whom to share their lives. This might mean single people and/or married couples choosing to live with one another in a community with a loosely agreed way of life. Or it might be as simple as the way you choose your flatmates.

How can the church support single people seeking to live a godly life?[9]

A full, contented single life does not just happen. It takes investment from the individual – but it should matter to the whole church too. Church leaders, in particular, have a responsibility to prepare and equip people to live well. Here are a few suggestions as to how:

1. Think of singleness as a way of life for all. We will all be single at one time, and probably more than once – especially at a time when people marry later in life and when so many marriages break up.

2. Churches should be places of healthy, appropriate physical touch and affection. In one survey, twice as many single people identified lack of touch as being one of the hardest things about being single, rather

---

[9]This section draws on some of the suggestions made by Kate Wharton in *Single Minded* (Oxford: Monarch, 2013), which I highly recommend.

than lack of sex. Our bodies are a good and beautiful part of how God has made us, and they need to be affirmed and loved through touch, not just words. How can we 'greet one another with a holy kiss' in our churches?

3. Nurture the expectation and possibility that single, and quite possibly married people, might consider living together in intentional communities, sharing their lives with one another in deep and seemingly shallow ways.

4. Teach biblically on the value of singleness, and practically on how to live a fulfilling and godly single life. By all means teach about godly dating and relationships, but teach about singleness in its own right too. Don't speak about singleness as a pre-marital state. Provide space for discussion of how this can be done well in your context (that will help you to hear from people what they need, too).

5. Don't imply that singleness is second best, even if you intend to be comforting. For example, 'It's not too late, you'll meet someone.' Comments like this are projections of your own aspirations for that person and assumptions of what is normal. They assume that the person is waiting for something else to happen, as opposed to enjoying life and serving God right now. Also, these platitudes might offer false hope leading to further disappointment.

6. Don't regularly ask after someone's relationship status. It would be rude if single people asked intimate questions about married couples. If they begin a relationship and they want you to know about it, they are perfectly

capable of telling you (or you'll see it on Facebook). Similarly, don't ask anyone why they don't have a boy/girlfriend or tell them they are a good catch. This is intended as a compliment but can makes things worse. There might be a really good reason why they aren't in a relationship (e.g. they just broke up with someone, they are not attracted to people of the opposite sex).

7. Be cautious about matchmaking – especially if you are introducing people to one another for the sake of it. Same-sex attracted people find this especially wearing. If you genuinely think two people might be suitable for one another, have a polite conversation with each of them first. They might not be interested in that person. Or they might not be looking for a relationship at the moment. Or they might be delighted. Take the trouble to find out what *they* think.

8. Don't assume that single people have lots more free time to serve in church or less stressful lives than married people.

9. Teach about good friendships and not just about sex and romantic relationships. When Gaby and I moved to London, we didn't know many people at first. At one point, she told me that she was feeling lonely. My pride was nettled. I protested, 'But I'm with you all the time! Aren't I enough for you?' Quite rightly, her answer was 'No!' She didn't just need a husband – she needed friends too.

10. Ensure that staff and leadership teams contain married and single people, and never assume that leaders need to be part of a couple.

11. Couples and families need to visit single people at home, and not just expect single people to come to them. It may seem easier for a single person to come to a family's home, but it deprives that person of the chance to welcome people into their own home and to offer hospitality.

12. If you are married, don't do everything as a couple – although it's not about having a token single person to hang around with out of pity either. It's about the heart behind your community and relationships: do you see community as something bigger and broader than your nuclear family? If so, it will be natural to include others, and it won't feel strained.

Conclusion

Singleness, like marriage, can be a hard road to walk. But it is not second best. Singleness, like marriage, needs intentional investment and support, if it is to be the fulfilling way of life that God intended it to be – namely, a beautiful witness to the way that we will all be in the new creation.

Go Deeper

Donald Goergen, *The Sexual Celibate* (Colorado Springs, CO: Image Books, 1979). Older, but still well worth a read.

William F. Kraft, *Whole and Holy Sexuality: How to Find Human and Spiritual Integrity as a Sexual Person* (Eugene, OR: Wipf and Stock, 1989).

Vaughan Roberts, *True Friendship: Walking Shoulder to Shoulder* (Leyland, Lancs: 10Publishing, 2013).

Ed Shaw, 'How can you live life without sex?' online at http://www.livingout.org/how-can-you-live-life-without-sex-.

Kathryn Wehr, *Singleness and the Early Church: Encouragement for Living the Single Life in Christ Today* (Cambridge: Grove Books, 2012).

Kate Wharton, *Single Minded* (Oxford: Monarch, 2013).

www.ingramcontent.com/pod-product-compliance
Lightning Source LLC
Chambersburg PA
CBHW070757050426
42452CB00010B/1878